# THE WAY IT IS

*Photographers and Writers*

Juan Arce

Jerry Banks

John Bruno

Jorge Cosme

Earl Eason

Henry Lorenzi

Ronald McClattie

William Parker

Jose Perales

Leonard Perry

Andre Rivera

Angel Rivera

Keith Roberson

Alonzo Smith

William Vega

# THE WAY IT IS

*Edited by John Holland*

Foreword by
J. Anthony Lukas

Harcourt, Brace & World, Inc.
New York

Curriculum-Related Books, selected and edited by
the School Department of Harcourt, Brace & World,
are titles of general interest for individual reading.

CDEFGHIJ

ISBN 0-15-294830-9

Library of Congress Catalog Card Number: 69-11495

Printed in the United States of America

## FOREWORD

In the aimless shuffle of a general-assignment reporter's routine, only rarely does a story reach out and touch him deeply. During my recent tour of duty in New York, one of these was the story of some boys from Brooklyn who learned to give form and meaning to their urban wasteland by looking through a camera's lens.

It hardly seemed promising that morning when an assistant city editor told me to "take a little trip out to Williamsburgh and see what they're doing at this school." The grimy Canarsie Line subway banged and rattled through the dusky morning, and out on Bushwick Avenue a gusty spring wind sent old newspapers and scraps of cardboards rasping through the gutters. The pockmarked face of the ancient schoolhouse gazed sadly down at me as I trudged in for what seemed then like just another "oh, how dreary life is in America's ghettos" story.

But there in the drafty principal's office I found not the weary, cynical teacher I had expected but a lively young man bristling with excitement about his new adventure in teaching. On the table in front of him were piles of photographs of the Williamsburg I had just walked through.

But as I began to leaf through them I found myself lifted out of the morning's bleakness and gradually caught up in the teacher's own excitement.

"That one there was taken by a boy who never done anything in school before," he was saying. "Nothing. An absolute zero up to then. But all of a sudden he's turned on. He loves his camera and he's even started writing about the pictures he takes.

"You can't imagine what a big thing this has been for these boys," he went on. "These were supposed to be kids who couldn't write. But now they're writing. This thing has given them at least one success under their belts, and after a life of so much failure, that can mean everything."

Then he led me upstairs to his classroom and introduced me to eight boys who were already impatiently pacing the room, shouting "Let's go," and "Come on, let's get this silly show on the road." They grabbed, tugged, fought for the shiny black Instamatic cameras which had been distributed, and then they loped out of the door and headed for a nearby high-school playground because "That's where the girls hang out."

The teacher warned each boy with one of the three precious cameras to take only six shots and then pass the equipment on to one of the others. But nobody stopped at six.

*Click* went the cameras as the boys passed a bum huddled asleep by a flaking brick wall; *click, click* they went as the class loped through the Bushwick freight yards, pulling the airbrakes as they gave off long hisses; *click, click, click* as they teetered on the edge above the raw sewage in Newtown Creek, watching a huge crane lift compressed auto wrecks onto a barge.

Back at the school an hour later, the boys handed in their film for development. They would see prints only a week later. "They say ghetto kids can't postpone pleasure, but what do you call this?" the principal asked.

*The Way It Is,* a collection of pictures and accompanying text by a class of boys at a Williamsburg school, may help to disprove some other pervasive myths about ghetto kids. It may also help to open up a wide range of new techniques in urban education. But if it does nothing else, it gives us a vivid glimpse of what it is like to grow up in a big city slum.

Credit should go to the Eastman Kodak Company which gave the original grant to set up this experimental project; to the Project in Educational Communication of the Horace Mann–Lincoln Institute of School Experimentation at Columbia University Teachers College, which supervised the program at nine New York schools; to teachers like John Holland, who carried it through in the classroom—but most of all to the boys themselves who took the pictures, wrote the text, and thereby allowed us to take a precious, if all too brief, look at the world through their eyes.

J. ANTHONY LUKAS

December 24, 1968

## EDITOR'S NOTE

A number of people helped with this book, directly and indirectly, both by working with the boys and by attempting to bring some of their achievements to the attention of the public. Those who stand out are Larry Lovett, who made so much equipment and so much of his time available; Dr. Louis Forsdale of Columbia University, whose grant from the Eastman Kodak Company financed a year-long photography project; Tom Mullee, who helped with the photographs during the year; and Elaine Carter, Violet Gordon, Ronald Hargett, and Ruth Simon, who were so skilled at collecting written material. My thanks to all of them.

JOHN HOLLAND

# THE WAY IT IS

This is a picture of slums.
Slums is a bad place to live.
Slums has no hot water sometimes.
Slums has insects in the house.
Slums has no lights in the hall sometimes.
Slums catch on fire fast.
The people who live
in the slums should move.

These are some of the guys who took the pictures and wrote the words in the book. All of us who did the book are in the seventh and eighth grades at Intermediate School 49 in the Williamsburg section of Brooklyn, New York.

Earl and Andre are climbing on the monkey bars in front of Bushwick Projects, where they live. You can tell it is winter because the trees don't have any leaves.

Henry, Willie, and Lenny are having fun having their picture taken. They are in the park outside I.S. 49, where a lot of kids hang out. Johnny is sitting in the fountain in the park, and Jose is standing beside him.

Another guy named Willie is in a
drugstore eating French fries and
waiting to order a soda. He keeps
pigeons on his roof.

Ronald and Jerry are leaning on a car trying to be cool. Ronald has a cigarette in his mouth, and he thinks that looks real bad. Jerry always likes to be leaning against something and smiling. He was getting ready to go to the city. Jerry and Ronald are such good friends, they're like brothers.

This is Angel, at Eastern District High School. The school looks like a castle. There are no broken windows, because there is a cop on every corner. Some people say Eastern District is for educated dumb-bells. Andre's brother dropped out in his second year. It's a good school to cut classes from, and some people think it's the worst school in Brooklyn. It's not though—it's not the toughest, either.

These kids are in front of Public School 250. The school was built in 1962, but look at the condition it's in already—broken windows, dirty walls, bent doors. After you make the city build a new school, they let it fall apart fast, and then they say people in the slums don't know how to take care of things.

This is Public School 132. It's a lot older than 250. More schools look like 132 than 250.

This is the door to Intermediate School 49. It's an old school too, and the windows over the door are broken. That's Angel, Juan, Johnny is behind Juan, and Andre. The lady is a school aide who patrols the halls. These guys decided to cut out of school and no one said anything because they thought they were taking pictures for class.

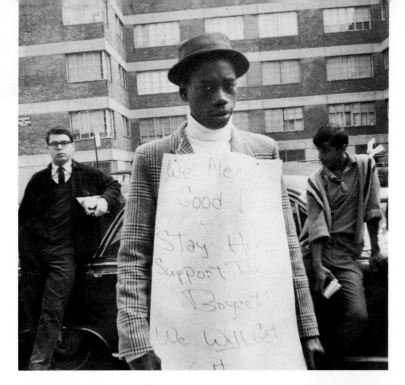

One day we had a boycott at school and a lot of kids didn't go in. Some of us were picketing outside because we wanted good books and things, and because we wanted better teachers. Not all the teachers are mean, but some of them are. It's not fair for them to be rough on kids just because they're bigger.

Here's a lonely guy waiting outside school with his books. He looks very bored, just waiting around. You spend a lot of time waiting around outside school in the morning if you get there early, or when you don't like a class or the teacher and you cut out for the period, or after school when there's nothing else to do.

These kids are cutting school, because it's boring and they don't understand the teachers. They got nothing to do but sit on a bench in the park next to I.S. 49 and watch people pass. They are scared they might get suspended if they cut too much, so they're going back into the school after the second period to eat lunch.

Here are some kids just waiting, and behind them is the door they sneak in and out of.

Andre and Gregory are dancing the "Tighten Up," but they'll get tired soon.

Raymond was just in a crap game and lost all his money, and now he's carving his name into a bench in the park. He seems to be very sad a lot, and he's always carving his name and his girl friend's name on benches. He thinks it's better being outside school than inside.

Boys from six to twenty-four years old hang out at 49 park, and they can learn anything real early. Mostly kids just play crap, sniff glue, drink wine, and smoke reefers. Almost every day you see these and other bad things. Instead of a school park, this has turned into a hangout with no supervision.

Some of these boys are Little Horsemen, a gang that hangs out in 49 park. A lot of kids around here belong in school, but they don't go.

A girl got too high sniffing Carbona and one of the Horsemen brought her coffee.

Some guys who hang out in 49 park beat up on people who don't belong there. When the cop comes they run, but they come right back. They steal clothes and candy, and they think they are big. Most of us don't like them. When you don't know them that good, they try to take your money, and they pull knives on you.

Here are Tata and Papo sitting on a bench; they are friends. Behind them are two guys drinking Gypsy Rose, getting high, and shooting dice. After they get high, they might mess with Tata and Papo. They are dropouts and they bother people. We hope Tata and Papo left after we took this picture, because we did.

If you get tired of sitting around in the park, you can play basketball or handball. In this picture we wanted to take a long shot of the basketball game, but Andre wanted to get in it so we told him to climb on the bar and we'd take the picture through him. He's in the group that's playing, but he's too short to play with them.

The 49 park is the only place the bigger kids play basketball, because the other parks are too small, and have only small kids. In the big park, they have big kids to play against. Here Alonzo just shot the ball, and it looks like he'll miss. Everyone is looking up hoping he doesn't get it in, because that will be the end of the game.

Angel is playing a game of handball and is looking back before he serves to see if the guy is ready. All the kids and even some of the teachers play handball. They got a fence around the park so when you serve the ball it doesn't go in the street. You can see Angel's shadow; it looks like a bulldog. His jacket is on the ground behind him, because they don't have anything to hang coats on in the park.

Jorge's sister Sonia is twelve years old. She's swinging with a girl friend at 49 park after three o'clock. School is out. Sonia doesn't cut, so she only comes to the park after school is out.

This is Ian up in a tree, acting like a monkey. It's a school day, but he looks happy just climbing around outside. You're always happy on a school day when you're outside.

Here's Earl again, sitting by himself in 49 park.

Earl has a big family, like most of the kids in Williamsburg. This is Earl's little brother Sam and his pet rabbit. He's four, and goes to pre-kindergarten. Sam likes to watch TV and play baseball with his sisters and his friends. He's the baby of the family, and whenever Earl goes someplace he likes to follow him. Earl's mother baby-sits for a neighbor, so the baby spends the day at her house and Sam has someone nearer his own age to play with.

Sometimes Earl's cousins and his friends come to stay overnight at his house. There are eight people living in a six-room house, but when cousins come, fitting in more is no problem if you're used to it. All the kids play together. Sometimes they get into fights, but they always

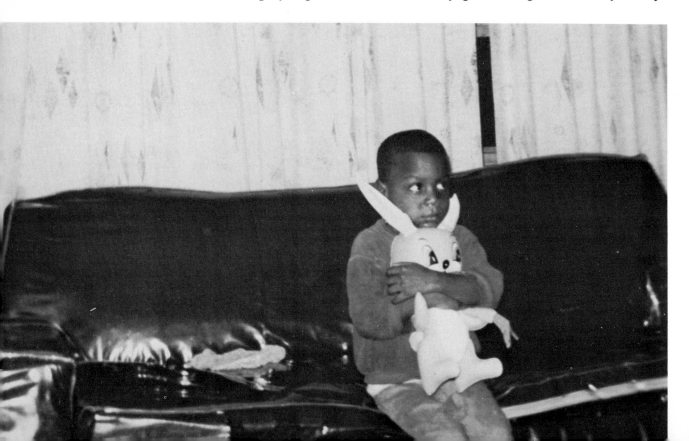

end up playing. Three cousins came to spend a few weeks, and their mother and father also came to visit. The two families live together even though Earl's cousins have a four-room apartment of their own in Manhattan. They have fun bunking together and both families live like one.

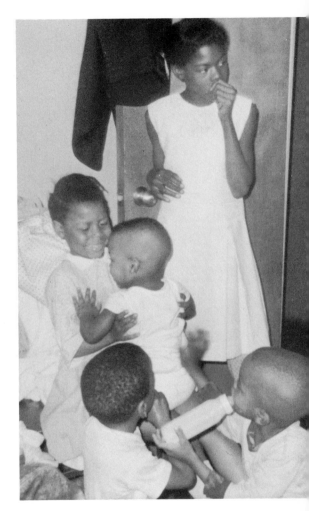

Johnny has a lot of relatives, too. This is his uncle, Tío. He's a nice guy and he likes to play with kids. He scares them and chases them all the time, and he makes strange sounds to get kids to laugh. When he heard Juan's name, he started saying, "Juan pan, coma pan." That means, "Juan is bread, eat the bread." Tío's not married. He lives with his mother. He's about twenty-eight years old. Tío goes to work on a bike. He's okay.

This is Lillian and a little girl named Juamo sitting in the grass in front of Bushwick Projects. The grass is Bushwick grass. Lillian's mother is Tati Vasquez, who is Andre's mother's best friend.

On Easter, Andre's sisters were dressed up and their mother wanted us to take a picture of them sitting on the grass, but the yard is mostly dirt. They don't have very much grass. So we made one stand up on a log, with the other one next to her, but you can still see the dirt. We wanted it to look like there wasn't any dirt, but there was too much.

This kid is named Junior. Junior always stays in his house. He never comes out because he can't walk. His legs are crippled. He's a nice guy. Everytime we used to see him we called him Buck Teeth Joe Junior. He liked it when we called him Buck Teeth, but then his mother heard about it and she said not to call him that any more, so now we call him Junior. Nobody plays with him, except sometimes they play records at his house and dance. He can't dance, so he just watches. He can only pull himself over to the window and look out. He has to hold himself up by his arms. He doesn't have a wheelchair, and he doesn't go to school. He can't read, and he can't talk good either. He looks like he felt happy about getting his picture taken. Sometimes people pay attention to him, but mostly they don't.

Here is Henry's friend Keith, standing in front of 140 Moore Street. The ring in the back is for the shower in summer.

Jorge's little brother is sitting on a turtle in Bushwick Park. He didn't have anyone to play with, but he looks happy. This is a cheap park because it hasn't got any pool or shower for the kids to cool off in.

This little girl is named Connie, and she is three years old. When you're eating something and she wants some, she'll take it and won't give it back. You can't blame her; you got to blame her mother. Connie is a nice girl. She has a new dress in her hand—she wanted to show everybody.

This little boy is standing on the sidewalk with no pants on. Maybe he can't afford pants. He's trying to act like he's not cold.

Doorsteps are a good place to talk to your friends, or play, or just sit. Jose and his friend are on a stairstep talking. Jose is the one with the white shirt and his friend has on a white jacket. They are in the doorway of a very old building where the guys hang out.

This girl just came from school. She is sitting down on a stairstep in the Williamsburg Projects. She looks glad to be home from school.

On Stagg Street these three kids were hiding from their mother because they took something that belonged to her and they were hiding it. One of them is Pojo, another one is Kique, and the girl in the middle is Maggie. They are happy kids.

These guys are across the street from I.S. 49. They are members of a gang in the neighborhood.

Juan is at the Williamsburg Projects with one of his girl friends and a baby. They are leaning on a car, and Juan and his girl friend are smiling and the baby is sucking a pacifier.

Willie was fooling around with two other guys. The one in front is doing Kung-Fu like Kato on "The Green Hornet."

These three kids were just having a good time on the street.

One day when we got bored just hanging around, we went to explore this old burned-out house. They have a lot of houses that nobody's supposed to live in, but winos and dope addicts sleep there. The first time we went in this house it had beds and mattresses, but they aren't there any more. When we looked through to the back, Andre didn't want to go, but Angel and some of us went and he followed us. We looked hard to be sure nobody was there.

In the back were a sink, old refrigerators, and a big wooden box.

Angel climbed up on them, and looked back to see if anybody was following us. When we went on the second floor, we went to a window to look out and see if any policeman was coming. You're not supposed to go in old buildings. When you're in a deserted house alone, you feel real scared, because you feel like somebody might jump you when you make the next turn.

On the second floor Angel found steps going to the top, and we climbed up on the roof. It was all little rocks and there were pieces of wood thrown around. When we saw there was nobody up there, Angel started fooling around and climbed on the chimney to look down, but it was scary. You could fall and get killed.

Why do kids go up on the roofs? You can see everything that's happening downstairs from the roof. When you look down at the people, they look like little ants. You can see cities, and Prospect Park, and get fresh air. And you can see the airplanes closer. Sometimes you go up on the roof just so you can get away from all the other people and be by yourself a little while.

Juan is trying to be big on the roof. He is always climbing to the highest trees in the park, so here he is on the highest roof. He thinks he's tough, touching the television antenna so the TV downstairs would get ruined. He almost fell when he touched it. Juan was going to throw something at Jorge, but he waited until he got his picture taken, then he threw the brick.

Jorge is on the roof because he wants to see everything all around.
He wants to see all the buildings in the world.

They always keep this roof clean, and it's a nice place to go, even when it's raining outside. When the sun is shining, you can come up here in your bathing suit and make like you're on the beach.

Sometimes kids go on the roof to do bad things, like sniff glue, because the cops don't come on the roof too often. Sometimes grownups take the needle there. People sleep on the roof. When Danny ran away from home, he slept on the roof. He slept there about an hour—then the cops caught him and took him home. Kids play tag, but it's danger-ous, because sometimes you fall.

Somebody fell down here and died. There was a kid named Pete sniffing glue on the roof with his friend James. Then some drug addicts came, and James ran when he saw them. He called to Pete, "Come on, here come two men." Pete said no, he wanted to stay on the roof. The junkies asked him for money, but he didn't have any money, only a ring that was real gold. So they took his ring and then they threw him off the roof. That's what some people think.

Other people think James did it, because he told us that night that he had a dream he pushed Pete off. But most people say it wasn't James, because he was Pete's friend. There are even some other people who think Pete died of glue and beer. They think he got poisoned.

They found out about Pete when a man saw him laying down there and called the cops. When they came, they thought he was drunk, so they didn't call the ambulance right away. When the ambulance did come, it was too late, and when he got to the hospital he was dead.

Everybody was crying. All of his friends collected money for the coffin, because Pete's parents didn't have enough to pay for it. At the funeral his father wanted to play records for him.

A lot of kids raise pigeons on the roofs and fly them. This kid is making a pigeon coop. Coops are fun to make. After he finishes, he's going to buy pigeons for it. He doesn't know how to fly them yet, but he's learning to.

Once Willie's brother had birds, but he sold them. One day the birds came back to the roof. Willie was up there and there wasn't any coop at all. He made one out of four milk boxes, and he kept the birds. It's fun to raise pigeons, and they look real nice when they fly high. To raise birds you have to know how to keep them in and how to mate them up. You have to feed them the right thing—grits, polished corn, and water—and you have to keep the coop clean and give the birds straw to make nests with.

You have to check the eggs to see if they are cracked. If the shell is cracked, the egg is no good, and you throw it away. You have to look for black eggs, because the baby pigeons come from the black eggs. When the eggs hatch, the birds feed the babies with their beaks. After a week you put yearbands on them. Then the birds start flying, and soon you mate them again. Sometimes you lose a lot of birds when people come on the roof and rob them. You can get money to buy more by selling any that are left to a pet store. When people buy them in the store and let them go, the birds come back home to their coop on your roof.

There are lots of dogs in the neighborhood, and they like to go on roofs too. Here's a dog we took up on the roof. This is a smart dog who listens to people if he knows them. He likes having his picture taken. You can tell, because when a dog stands like that he must be posing for pictures.

Angel's dog's name is Negrita—that means Blackie. He takes her on the roof because the kids on the street tease her and she bites them.

Every time she gets on the roof, she runs around real quick to see if anybody's there. If she found somebody, she'd start barking. After she looks all over the roof, she stops running, smells around, and starts to play. She likes to look at things from the roof, because they all look different from up high.

There's a lot of wild dogs too, and some of them are real mean. There's one we call Bullet because he can run fast, and he has a girl friend we call Brownie. Tramp is a boxer. He's named Tramp because he can beat up all the other dogs.

This is Donald playing with a dog called Lucky in the back yard. He's a nice dog that doesn't bite. Donald took the dog and lifted him to his hind legs and Lucky liked it.

Here's another beat-up back yard with all sorts of things in it like garbage, wine bottles, and rats. See the toy dog? That means a kid must have been playing there. Some people live in places like this and they can't do any better. It's a bummy place. In the background there is a co-op project named the Lindsay Park Houses. They built the co-op right in the middle of the slums.

Streets and sidewalks in the slums are dirty and cracked, and the houses are all beat up. These houses have signs and all kinds of paint on them. They have old doors to hold them up, but they look like they're ready to fall down. In the back, on a wall between two windows, a sign says Gold Medal Flour. There must have been a factory there once.

This is the door to 140 Moore Street, in the Bushwick Projects. It's a nice place to live because it's newer and cleaner.

There isn't much room inside an apartment to do things, so Fred is fixing his bike on the sidewalk. It's lucky for this picture the garbage man finally came, because there was garbage all over the place just an hour before. Most apartments are very small and in the summer they get hot like an oven, so people do a lot of things outside. They sit on the stoops to talk, play dominoes, fix things, and see their friends. Sometimes a cop chases you when you're sitting on the stoop, even though you're not doing anything wrong.

When it gets hot, everyone likes to go to Coney Island beach. It's usually very crowded in the summer—so many people you hardly got room to sit down. The only reason it isn't crowded here is that it was cold that day.

If you can't go to the beach when it's too hot, you can open a johnny pump like Keith and Alonzo are doing. You've got to be careful, though, because a cop will chase you if he sees you. Alonzo's watching to see if anybody is coming.

It sometimes takes two people because the johnny pump sticks.

When you finally get it on, the water comes slow at first, but if you turn it on all the way it goes real hard and cold. You can take a can and knock the bottom out of it and use it to shoot the water in the air. We try to hit cars that have got their windows open. The best thing is a car with the top down.

After you fool around for a while, you get in the water and get wet and cool. It feels nice. Even girls like to get wet. They get hot in the summer too.

Sometimes we walk around and look at the stores. The stores in the neighborhood sell almost everything. In the flower store you buy statues and flowers for dead people. It's across the street from Holy Trinity Church. You can also get presents for birthdays, graduations, and other times.

The Moore Street food market is a big indoor market that the city owns and rents to different people. It's called the Red Market because it's red outside. It's a block long and sells mostly Spanish fruits and vegetables. This man is cutting up yautías —that's like a yam. To the right of them are ñames, and hanging up are plátanos.

On the same block as the Red Market there are outdoor stores selling clothes, fruits, material, shoes, and toys. They are always having sales and each one is always trying to undersell the others. But they always make sure they get the money from the suckers—us.

74

Henry is looking in a store window at all the toys. They cost a lot of money.

After school Willie goes to work in this chicken market. First he goes into the office and gets his apron, and then he goes to the front, where they kill the chickens. To kill a chicken, you take it by the wings, grab its neck, and squeeze the neck until it breaks. Then you take a knife and cut its throat until the windpipe shows, and then you throw him in the barrel so the blood will drip out. After the chicken gets killed, he jumps all over the barrel. Later you take him to the back and put him in a machine that takes all the feathers off. Willie kills everything there—chickens, rabbits, roosters, and ducks. They kill everything except rabbits the same way. To kill a rabbit, you hold him by the back feet, pick up a stick they call the bat, and hit him on the head once or twice. When the rabbit stops kicking, he gets put in the back. Willie says the job is all right—he doesn't mind it and the pay isn't bad. But he doesn't know if he'll keep working there. The smell bothers his nose.

This stolen car was found close to the market. Some guys wrecked it and took the parts, and then they set the car on fire. Sometimes kids steal cars to go for fun rides, and sometimes dope addicts steal cars and take the parts. They sell the parts for money to buy drugs. Sometimes people leave their cars because they ran out of gas, and when guys see a strange car on the block they strip it and sell everything. When kids see a strange car, they just jump on it and play in it. They are bored, and this is something to do.

Old cars stay on the streets sometimes for six months before they are taken away. This old wreck says "car service" on the front. Real taxis don't come around here very much because they are afraid, so there are these car services that are really taxis without taxi licenses.

These two women aren't looking for anything out the window—
they're just looking. People look out the windows a lot at what's going
on in the street. They can gossip about what they see other people
doing, or they can call their kids or their friends, or they can just keep
watching for something interesting to happen.

You can see a lot of different kinds of people around here. This guy is always hanging around. Maybe he used to have a job, but now he never seems to have anything to do, because he just leans on the front of a building. Maybe he makes faces at you because he isn't happy.

This old lady stands outside a lot. Anybody she sees, she always stops and talks to them, whether she knows them or not. When she talks to you and you don't pay any attention, she puts her hand on her heart.

This is a guy who works in our school. Before he worked in our school he was a boxer in the Army—that's what he told us. When he was telling us, he was demonstrating with Alonzo Smith. If you say anything about his mother, he'll chase you around the whole school.

These bums are by the Red Market, where they stay. It's a street of bums. People wonder what makes a man a bum. We wonder ourselves sometimes. Maybe they had good jobs before they became bums but got fired because they drank too much. Most of us think they all had problems before they got to be bums. Sometimes they work in the Red Market, emptying garbage to get a few pennies to buy wine. In the summer they sleep in the street, but in the winter they sleep in halls, old cars, and project staircases. People always call the police when bums come to sleep around their houses. Bums ought to be helped, though, not bothered. These three bums are drinking, having a good time with the wine, thinking what to do next.

Another day one of them is on the corner, hustling money to buy wine.

This bum is laying down, having a dream about what to do tomorrow.

Sometimes we wonder what we'll be doing, too. The guys don't talk about it a lot but we think about it sometimes, because where do you go from here?